GO

but not
forgotten

By A. J. Ludlam & P. J. Eldridge.
Published by the Lincolnshire Wolds Railway Society

**A very dapper looking Alfred Mitchell,
stationmaster at Halton Holgate in the late 1920s.**

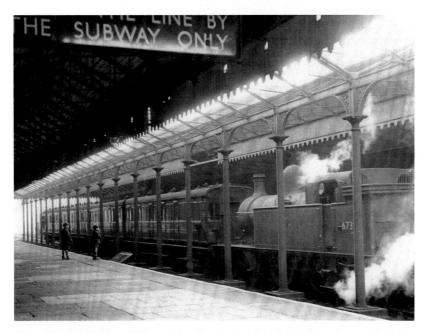

Class C12 4-4-2T No 67398 with the Quad Articulated set of coaches used on the services between Louth and Grimsby has just arrived under the overall roof with a train from Grimsby on 27th October 1951. Note the notice board advising passengers to "Cross by the subway only". *N. Stead.*

ISBN 978-0-9926762-0-9

The Lincolnshire Wolds Railway Society would like to thank Alf Ludlam and Phil Eldridge for giving their time to compile this publication, and to Allinson Print & Supplies for their support with the project.

Printed by Allinson Print & Supplies, Allinson House, Lincoln Way, Fairfield Industrial Estate, Louth, Lincolnshire LN11 0LS

Issue 1. Autumn 2013.

CONTENTS

Class J6 0-6-0 No 64214 of Boston Shed approaches Halton Holgate station with the daily pick-up goods train on 22nd November 1958, the month of its final closure. By this time the station had lost its wooden canopy. *H. Davies.*

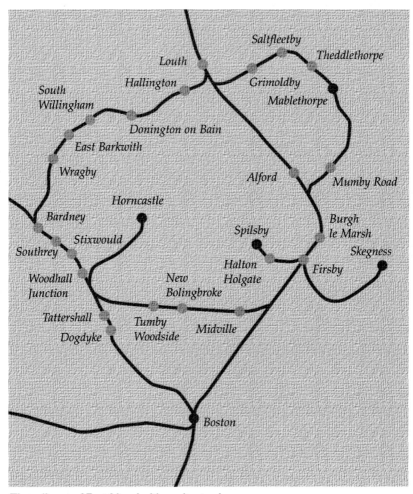

The railways of East Lincolnshire prior to closure.
The stations covered in this book are highlighted in green.

INTRODUCTION

The first railway in Lincolnshire was opened by the Midland Railway, running between Nottingham and Lincoln St Marks, on 3rd August 1846.

Within the next three years 200 miles of track had been laid in the county. By 1877 almost 500 miles of railways had been constructed, amounting to three quarters of the eventual provision.

Since the 1950s almost two thirds of the county's network has closed. However, many station buildings still survive and photographs of them in their original settings are invaluable and a testament to a lost rich heritage. The quality and substantial nature of these buildings is no doubt one of the reasons why they have survived so well.

We would like to thank the current owners of the featured stations for allowing us to photograph them as they are today and for their enthusiasm for our little project.

Alf Ludlam.

C12 No 67379 stands at the idyllic East Barkwith station (which is still extant) on the Louth-Bardney line on 13th October 1951, less than a month prior to its closure to passenger traffic. *P. Wells.*

HALLINGTON signal box in Great Northern days, including the signalman and platelaying gang which was based at nearby Withcall station. *Peter Chapman Collection.*

HALLINGTON station looking east in the 1890s, with the station staff and stationmaster's family in attendance. *Peter Chapman Collection.*

The Louth to Bardney branch

HALLINGTON

Hallington, 2 miles south west of Louth, had a population of 112 in 1881. The Lord of the Manor was Henry Chaplin and the stationmaster was James Chambers.

Bob Dale's father had a well-established large farm in the Binbrook area. In 1940 the Ministry of Agriculture began telling farmers to grow certain crops which were in short supply. Farmer Dale decided to move his farm closer to a railway, making his sugar beet crop more profitable as it cost only 4/6d a ton delivered to Bardney by rail compared to 6/- by road. He took a farm near Hallington.

The Reverend Wyer-Honey of Raithby would collect his "Daily Telegraph" and "Times" newspapers from the station at 8.20 am. He also used the line to transport two or three of his hunting horses to meets at Hainton, Wragby and Willingham.

Train crews out of Louth used to like a full head of steam in order

HALLINGTON. Just to the east of Hubbards Hills, Louth, where the Louth to Bardney line crossed the road to Raithby. It is possible to walk the trackbed from here to Withcall and get an idea of the steepness of the incline.

to tackle the stiff incline all the way to the middle of Withcall Tunnel. The 7.00 am out of Louth would whistle at Hallington Distant signal, giving the stationmaster time to get the gates open and catch the papers as they were thrown from the train. If the gates were not open and the train had to stop the air turned blue!

A forlorn looking Hainton & South Willingham station in August 1953 - two years after closure to passengers but still open for goods traffic. *Douglas Thompson.*

SOUTH WILLINGHAM AND EAST BARKWITH

South Willingham, a pleasant village on the acclivity of a picturesque valley 5 miles north east of Wragby, had a population of 300 in 1881. Edward Heneage MP was Lord of the Manor and Charles Smith stationmaster.

East Barkwith, situated 3 miles north east of Wragby, had a population of 339 in 1881. J Overton, the carrier, worked to Market Rasen on Tuesdays, Lincoln on Fridays and Horncastle on Saturdays. George Prentice was the stationmaster.

In 1944 a train of 18 wagons, each loaded with one large bomb in the charge of a class J11 0-6-0, was delivering bombs to stations on the line. The first station at which wagons were detached was South Willingham. The engine went forward with five wagons, leaving the rest and the brake van on the single main-line, the engine coupled up five empty wagons in the siding intending to back them onto the rest of the train. However, all that could be seen was the rest of the train disappearing down the incline in the direction of East Barkwith.

The runaway train ran through East Barkwith station and demolished the crossing gates. Fortunately communication had been established with the signalman at Wragby who was able to open his crossing gates. He estimated the speed of the wagons at 40 mph as they passed through the station. The train finally came to a rest in Kingthorpe Bottom, see-sawing itself to a standstill. The train crew and staff at South Willingham feared that the runaway would collide with the Lincoln-Louth pick-up goods train, due on the branch at the time. Fortunately the train was still at Bardney. The guard was held responsible for not securing the brakes on the train.

HAINTON & SOUTH WILLINGHAM station today. The brick base for the signal box, seen in the picture opposite, is still in situ in the garden, as is the well which supplied the station's water.

EAST BARKWITH station in 1951, showing the booking office, the stationmaster's house, the lamp room and the slope of the cattle dock. The station clock and its canopy, a feature of stations on this line, is seen next to the door of the booking office. *Mike Black.*

EAST BARKWITH is little changed from when it was an operational station, the platform edge is clearly seen and the distinctive pine trees are still in evidence to the right.

DONINGTON-ON-BAIN

Donington-On-Bain lies in the valley of the River Bain, 7 miles from Louth and 8 from Wragby. It is sheltered by some of the highest hills in the Lincolnshire Wolds. In 1881 the population numbered 473. Charles Freeborough was stationmaster here for over a quarter of a century.

During World War 2, 233 Maintenance Unit had several railheads along the branch to supply armaments to the nearby airfields. Wragby, South Willingham, Donington-On-Bain and Withcall were used. Hallington was used as an empties dump, from where assembled empty cases would be returned to the munitions factories.

233 Maintenance Unit had a bomb dump on the old Roman road

DONINGTON-ON-BAIN station seen from the road overbridge in April 1951, seven months prior to closure to passengers. The station buildings are constructed of red brick with courses of buff brick decoration. Immediately next to the wooden store on the right is the gent's urinal, attached to the stationmaster's house with its impressive bay window, beyond which is the single storey booking office and waiting room. The sidings ran behind the station building controlled by the signal box on the extreme left. Donington-On-Bain was on the most beautiful section of the branch between Withcall and Wragby. *Mike Black.*

between Caistor and Horncastle, known as "bomb alley", it was guarded by soldiers with fixed-bayonets at every road junction.

Most of the bombs were delivered to Donington-On-Bain which was well situated in a valley between two tunnels, a quiet wayside station well equipped with sidings. The bombs came in all shapes and sizes, from little four pounders to the giant 20,000 lb block-busters.

Mr Jones, stationmaster at Donington-On-Bain during the war, said they often had two special bomb trains arrive at the station a day, sometimes more, "we dealt with thousands upon thousands of them".

DONINGTON-ON-BAIN station today. In the picture is resident Colin Hutson who has lived at the Station House since 1970 and remembers travelling to Louth on the train when he was a teenager. The shape of the single storey brick built building that stood to the east of the stationmaster's house can just be discerned by the slightly lighter brickwork at the near end of the house.

WRAGBY

In 1881 Wragby was a small market town with a population numbered at 508. Situated $10^{1}/_{2}$ miles east of Lincoln and 10 miles north of Horncastle at the junction of turnpikes from these places and from Louth and Market Rasen. Two annual fairs were held on 1st May for sheep and 28th and 29th September for horned cattle, both of them a busy time for the railway. Coal merchants using the station included Amos Bratley and William Epton. This was the only station on the branch with two platforms. Thomas Saggers was stationmaster here in 1881 and remained in place for over 40 years.

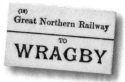

(16)
Great Northern Railway
TO
WRAGBY

Wragby Station.

WRAGBY station in Great Northern Railway days with the tall figure of the stationmaster Thomas Saggers and his staff on the platform, taken from the level crossing. The second platform with its basic waiting shelter can be seen, so too the signal box which controlled the sidings that ran behind the second platform. Although almost identical in style to the buildings at Donington-On-Bain the ones at Wragby were built of buff coloured bricks with courses of red bricks as decoration.

WRAGBY station today looks very tidy, with its station lamp and British Railways enamel sign proclaiming 'Wragby' on the end wall.

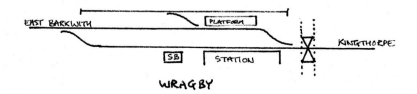

EAST BARKWITH

PLATFORM

SB   STATION

KINGTHORPE

WRAGBY

The Firsby to Spilsby branch

HALTON HOLGATE was the intermediate station on the Firsby to Spilsby branch line. The four mile line was opened on 1st May 1868 and closed to freight on 30th November 1958. Halton Holgate had a stationmaster, two porters and four platelayers.

In the 1920s Walt Hickman took a farm near the station. He set fruit trees in rows about twenty yards apart and between them he set thousands of spring flowering bulbs. Ernest Borrill recalled his mother going strawberry picking, starting at 4.00 am until 7.00am, when she would return home to get the two children their breakfast and off to school. She went back to the fields returning home again at midday to see to her husband and children's dinner, before returning and working until 5.00 pm. The fruit and flowers were loaded onto

HALTON HOLGATE station from the road overbridge in June 1950. The goods shed and yard, including the coal drops, are beyond the station. *Mike Black.*

the train at Halton Holgate at 9.40 am and transferred to the Kings Cross train at Firsby, reaching London at 12.25 pm, it couldn't happen now, so much for progress!

Joe Shaw, the butcher at Halton Holgate, would take the train to Boston each Wednesday, returning at 4.30 pm. At the rear of the train was a cattle wagon containing a bullock. The wagon was shunted off at Halton Holgate and the beast driven up to the Shaw's premises. The family would sit down for their meal and afterwards slaughter the bullock. It was sold on the rounds on Friday and Saturday, there were no fridges in those days to store fresh meat.

HALTON HOLGATE today. Seen from the same road overbridge the station retains its original character, except for the addition of the conservatory, which stands on the trackbed of the branch. The goods shed is visible in the distance.

The East Lincolnshire Main Line

LOUTH is situated at a point where the Lincolnshire Wolds meet the Marsh. It owed its growth to its position as an important market town. Some attempts were made to bring the industrial revolution to the town in the late 18th century when a canal was opened from Tetney Haven in 1770. In the mid-19th century there was much activity on the canal dealing with coal and wood and also Adam Eve's wool and carpet factories. However the town was too remote for a future based upon industry, the factories only employing a tiny number of people, most earning their livings serving the needs of the surrounding countryside.

The foundation stone of Louth station was laid by Miss Charlotte Pye, the 16 year old daughter of Henry Pye, a Director of the East Lincolnshire Railway Company, on 8th July 1847.

The completed building was in a handsome neo-Jacobean style, with curved stone capped gables, a balustraded roof with linked chimney stacks and a superb stone, round arched, porte-cochere with Renaissance details. The platform side was, unusually, constructed of white brick. A stationmaster's house was added a few years later very much in the style of the original building. All in all it was one of the handsomest buildings on the GNR system.

The impressive frontage of Louth station in the 1930s. *Douglas Thompson.*

A bay platform was constructed at the south end to coincide with the opening of the Mablethorpe branch for the use of branch trains to there and to Bardney. The south end was resignalled and South signal box built in 1887. The original footbridge at the south end was replaced by a passenger subway, a unique way of crossing the line in Lincolnshire.

For many years Louth was an important centre of railway operations in Lincolnshire, it had motive power, engineering and signalling departments based at the station.

After closure of the line the station suffered badly. Internally it was wrecked by vandals, the ball finials pushed off the main entrance and window frames wrenched from their sockets. An application to demolish it was made on 27th March 1987 and was thankfully rejected. The station survives in a modified form, a testiment to a time when one in five Ludensians worked for the railway.

LOUTH station. The beautiful proportions of the station and its splendid portico are seen to good advantage in this shot. It went through some very hard times after closure of the railway but has thankfully survived.

A Class 31 diesel alongside Louth North signal box in 1979. *Malcolm Roughley.*

LOUTH NORTH SIGNAL BOX was built in 1890 and stands at what once was Keddington Road level crossing and the northern entrance to Louth station environs.

The box survived the closure of the line in 1980 and was for a while the headquarters of the Louth branch of the Grimsby-Louth Railway Preservations Society. At present it is a private dwelling occupied by the family of an LWR volunteer.

Louth North box today.

LEGBOURNE ROAD on 2nd December 1970 after closure of the line.

LEGBOURNE ROAD station was an early casualty, closing to passenger traffic on 7th December 1953. The station house and goods shed was once run as a railway museum by Mike Legge. The signal box in the picture below stood originally at Tramway Crossing on the Mablethorpe Loop at a spot where the railway crossed the trackbed of the 2' 6" gauge Alford & Sutton Tramway (1884-89).

LEGBOURNE ROAD station today.

FIRSBY station stood in stark contrast to the surrounding area, a solid, impressive man-made statement, contrasting with the empty countryside in which it stood. Built in 1848 as

part of the ELR between Boston and Grimsby, it later became an important junction with links to Spilsby and Skegness. There was an impressive ornate entrance to the station leading to an L-shaped booking office and waiting room. Its main platforms were linked by an overall roof, similar to that at Louth. Next to the waiting room was a well-equipped refreshment room heated by the stations own gas supply. Platform 2 had two waiting rooms with gas fires and platform 3 was unroofed and used by Skegness trains. An impressive goods shed with recessed blank windows on one side and arched windows on the other was situated north of the station.

A legendary stationmaster at Firsby was Joe Toplis, whose dealings with the public were not always polite. On one occasion a gentleman's hatless head appeared at a carriage window as Joe was shouting "Over the bridge, Skegness over the Bridge". "Hey mister,

The view from the footbridge at Firsby station looking south on 25th May 1970. The level-crossing was furnished with unusual overlapping gates. To the left the track leaves the Skegness platform and to the right the Spilsby branch left the main line via the turnout beyond the signal box. *Gordon Brown.*

I've lost me 'at", interrupted the agitated passenger. "Then keep your ruddy head inside!"

On another occasion Joe was attending a Grimsby train and was about to give the "right away" to the guard, when a lady passenger alighted and asked Joe what time she would arrive in Grimsby, "Get inside missus, you'll be there nearly as soon as the train!"

FIRSBY Crossing Keeper's house still remains at what was an important junction station, with connections to Skegness, Spilsby, Grimsby and Boston.

BURGH-LE-MARSH station had parallel platforms, all the main offices, goods shed, small crane, large cattle dock and signal box were on the up side. Immediately north of the station a level-crossing crossed the main road to Burgh-le-Marsh village and Skegness.

During World War 2 two railmounted 12" howitzers were based on the ELR. They spent some time at Burgh-le-Marsh and Willoughby stations. The guns had a range of eight miles, but were never used in anger. A trial firing from Willoughby smashed all the windows in the station and brought tiles off the roofs of nearby houses, a firing from Burgh-le-Marsh brought down an ceiling at nearby Gunby Hall, after which firings ceased.

The station buildings and goods shed survive and include the signal box, which can be seen where the road crosses the site of the former level crossing. For many years the Goods shed formed part of Alan and Sheila Turner's Lincolnshire Railway Museum.

BURGH-LE-MARSH taken from Skegness Road, with the full complement of the station and yard staff. The goods shed stands beyond the station platform.

BURGH-LE-MARSH today. A display of enamel signs on the end wall of the station building make an impressive display. Out of sight at the far end of the building is the signal box next to what was the level crossing over the A158 Skegness road.

ALFORD station building was similar to that at Firsby in style, with a three arched portico entrance leading in to a passageway which led to the platform. The passageway included the entrance to a large parcels office and the ticket window and accompanying office. Turning right on the platform there was the general waiting room, a store room, the stationmaster's office and a residence, at one time occupied by Mr Hardwick, a porter and lorry driver. The overall roof was replaced by a canopy after World War 2. The position of the signal box near the level crossing, at the north end, caused some heavy lever movements due to its distance from the points it operated.

The station yard had a loading dock, a goods shed which could take nine wagons and contained Harrison's grain store in its upper storey. The shed and a 15 ton crane were blown up during World War 2, causing the death of the only person killed in Alford during the hostilities, shunt-horse driver Bush, who was on fire watch at the time.

The southern end of Alford station in GNR days complete with its overall roof. The southbound train of six-wheeled carriages is drawn by a GNR class 264 2-2-2 engine built by Sturrock, No 266. The engine was rebuilt by Stirling in 1873 and withdrawn in 1899. *Stewart Neil.*

The approach and entrance to Alford station.

ALFORD station portico, which was similar to the one at Firsby, now acts as the entrance to Jackson's Building Supplies showroom, the road appropriately named 'Beeching Way'.

Removing track between Coningsby and Woodhall Junction in October 1970. The River Witham is on the right. *R. B. Wilkinson.*

Track lifting on the Louth-Bardney line in June 1961. *Mike Black.*

The Lincolnshire Loop

The River Witham has its whole course in Lincolnshire, at Lincoln it became navigable, flowing in a south easterly direction to Boston and the sea. It was along the banks of the Witham that the Great Northern Railway decided to build the Boston to Lincoln section of their Lincolnshire loop line, which ran from Peterborough via Spalding, Boston and Lincoln to Gainsborough, and on to Doncaster.

Many stations along the Witham section had an unusual Italianate style station house, with a tall three storey tower with windows with semi-circular arches. They had particularly large chimney blocks and chamfered overhanging roofs. Yellow brick predominated at all stations except Woodhall Junction, where they were used to provide a decorative alternative to the red brick building.

DOGDYKE station seen here in **GNR** days with the signal box, the Italianate tower of the stationmaster's house and the goods shed all seen to good advantage.

Sinclair's siding at the station served a mill and coal yard, the firm had a solid tyred Model T Ford lorry, which ran between the siding and their headquarters in the nearby village of New York. Mr Grainger, who ran the store in New York, cycled to Dogdyke station each Wednesday morning to catch the 8.00 am train to Boston. He would travel with a Gladstone bag chained to his wrist. In Boston he would purchase goods for the New York shop, bringing the lighter portable goods back with him. The rest of the merchandise would be collected by Bert Eyre on Thursday.

Bert started working at the shop aged fourteen. One of his duties was to collect the local and national newspapers from the station. These would be sorted at the station and deliveries made along the route back to the shop. The papers would be signed for at the station. At the time Bert was learning Italic handwriting and on a visit to the station to collect the papers his signature was refused because "it wasn't joined up writing".

The Model T Ford lorry was used for fetching items such as vinegar, paraffin and general groceries - eggs and butter for example, for the shop. It also collected a five ton load of salt from the station which was used for salting meat in the days before refrigeration.

The level crossing at Dogdyke station gave access to the "Packet Inn", which, in 1856 was run by James Sampson, who also operated the ferry. Seen here are three types of crossing vessels, the largest could carry a horse and cart. The smaller one beyond and the punt in the foreground, just people. This photo gives a good idea of just how close to the river the railway ran.

TATTERSHALL'S Italianate buildings are well seen in the photo opposite, note the substantial chimney block and the chamfered overhanging roof.

Beet, potatoes, corn and wool were loaded here. Sacks would be hired from the railway company, the weight of the sack being determined by its contents: 19 stones for beans or peas, 18 stones for wheat, 16 stones of barley and 12 stones of oats. These would be manhandled - Fleeces were made into "bales" or "sheets" stitched together with heavy wooden pegs, each "sheet" holding 40 fleeces and were hauled onto farm wagons using wooden planks for their journey to the station.

TATTERSHALL station today. The elegant lines of the station house, now the home, studios and gallery of artists Arthur and Gwen Watson.

The original name, Kirkstead, was changed to WOODHALL JUNCTION on 10th July 1922. The 1855 buildings were added to in 1855 for the opening of the Horncastle branch, a bay was built for the use of the branch line trains from which they reversed to gain the junction before going forward onto the branch.

On the down platform a small waiting shelter stood next to a cast iron gents urinal, which is now preserved at the Museum of Lincolnshire Life, in Lincoln.

In the 1930s three or four poultry packers worked in the area. They travelled around in what was the forerunner of the modern pick-up truck, with wooden crates in the back. During the morning they would buy live poultry, kill, pluck and dress the birds and despatch them by rail to Smithfield Market in London.

Opposite top: Lincoln based class B1 4-6-0 No 61281 arrives at Woodhall Junction with the 9.15am Lincoln to Skegness passenger train on 29th April 1954. On the down platform can be seen the cast iron gent's urinal and the splendid station nameboard. *H. Casserley.*

The impressive Italianate tower and station buildings at Woodhall Junction are now the home of broadcaster and railway enthusiast Alan Stennett.

SOUTHREY station waiting shelter, signal box, the station house set at right-angles to the track and the distinctive concrete station nameboard, a scene little changed over the course of its 122 years of active life. Seen here in August 1970 two months before the line closed. Over the level crossing to the left was the River Witham where a ferry operated connected to the White Horse Inn on the opposite bank.

Percy Carter remembered moving from Tattershall to Southrey in January 1937. "Our furniture should have been taken to Southrey by a goods train from Boston. However owing to a derailment at Langrick the train was cancelled and we finished up sleeping on the floor for our first night at Southrey." *Peter Grey.*

SOUTHREY station is now a stop-off point for cyclists on the Water Rail Way from Boston to Lincoln.

STIXWOULD had a layout similar to that at Southrey, except for a slight difference in the arrangement of the platform shelters. The two-storey station house stood at right-angles to the track, gable ended with decorative barge boards and upper floor windows also gabled. The site was completed by a signal box and goods yard. Drinking water and paraffin for the station were delivered by rail.

When the station lost its stationmaster and came under the authority of the stationmaster at Woodhall Junction, the station house was occupied by the signalman and his wife. They also operated the ferry across the Witham, which was capable of carrying motor vehicles, and sold food and cigarettes to anglers who came to fish the river. *Peter Grey.*

STIXWOULD station today. The house has been extended so that it now incorporates the signal box.

BARDNEY

The first railway to arrive at Bardney was the Lincolnshire Loop line in 1848. The station was a through station, a station house of the "Italianate" style, featured along the line, a goods shed and sidings. With the appearance of the Louth & Lincoln Railway in 1876 Bardney became a junction station, with a new signal box and platform added to the double-line junction. Bardney was a very busy station dealing with trains serving the nearby sugar factory and Morrell's canning factory, just west of the level-crossing, as well as trains off the Louth-Bardney branch and Boston and Lincoln trains. After the gradual closure of the Boston-Lincoln line in the early 1970s, the only section to remain open was that between Lincoln and Bardney, which was singled and, effectively, became a branchline serving the sugar factory with trips "as required". This section was finally lifted in 1983.

The splendid station nameboard on the island platform at Bardney in June 1951.
Mike Black.

BARDNEY station showing the "Italianate" stationmaster's house, the adjoining platform served trains off the Louth-Bardney branch, the island platform Boston-Lincoln trains. The turnout just beyond the water column on the right led to the sugar factory.

Sadly very little remains of the railway at Bardney but the Station Heritage Centre and Tearoom, with its superb collection of local railway memorabilia, is a reminder of times past. One notable survivor is the station nameboard mounted on the wall, which can also be seen in the 'past' photo on the left. The Heritage Centre is a popular refreshment break for cyclists using the Water Rail Way and even sells fish and chips from an original British Railways brakevan!

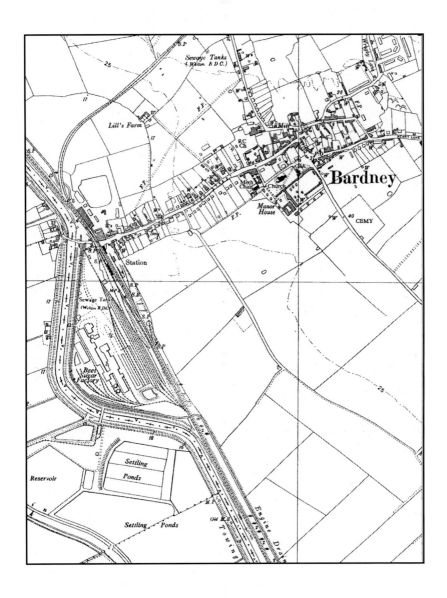

An **Ordnance Survey map of Bardney station** showing how closely the railway followed the **River Witham between Boston and Lincoln.** The sugar beet factory and its complex of sidings stand in the bend of the river opposite the station. The Louth to Bardney branch line runs in from the top of the map.

The Louth & East Coast Line

The Louth and East Coast Railway left the East Lincolnshire Railway at Mablethorpe Junction, just south of Louth and ran for eleven miles single track to Mablethorpe. It opened on 16th October 1877 and was known as "The Farmers Line". Although it did carry some holiday traffic its greatest benefit was the conveyance of farm produce and animals to and from the Louth Cattle and Fat Stock Market, one of the foremost of this kind of market in the country.

On 23rd September the Sutton and Willoughby Railway opened, running from Willoughby on the East Lincolnshire Railway seven miles to Sutton-on-Sea. An extension from Sutton-on-Sea to Mablethorpe completed the loop and was opened on 14th July 1888.

The Louth-Mablethorpe section closed on Saturday 3rd December 1960. The southern section was a victim of Beeching's recommendations and closed on 3rd October 1970, a bleak day for Lincolnshire railways.

THEDDLETHORPE stationmaster and signalman witness the arrival of a passenger train in the charge of **GNR class F2 0-4-2 mixed traffic engine No 951.** The stationmaster's house bay window and a weighing machine can be seen on the platform.

THEDDLETHORPE was the smallest station on the line with a single platform and a siding. Jack Lingard lived in Theddlethorpe St Helen in the early 1900s and remembered the railway being used as a walkway, "Walking along the railway saved time and shoe leather. A man called George was killed whilst walking the line near Theddlethorpe. He was stone deaf and couldn't hear the approach of the train or its whistle.

When we moved to Grimsby in 1919 the railway company ran 1/-return trips from time to time. They ran to Mablethorpe but we got off at Theddlethorpe to walk along the beach."

Almost identical to Grimoldby and Saltfleetby stations on the Louth to Mablethorpe line, Theddlethorpe still retains its railway character.

SALTFLEETBY too had a single platform and two sidings. Saltfleetby resident Mrs Annie Lowry, aged 96, had travelled on the first train on the line in 1877 but, due to the cold weather, could not make the final trip on the line in 1960.

GRIMOLDBY station buildings were similar to those at Theddlethorpe and Saltfleetby, and all were similar to those on the Louth-Bardney branch. Constructed of red brick with courses of buff bricks used as decoration, all had a brick built bay window on the stationmaster's house. The signal boxes on the north section of the loop were all of GNR wooden construction. The boxes were block posts only, serving sidings and controlling the level crossings. The Louth-Mablethorpe section was controlled by staff and ticket and the Willoughby-Mablethorpe by electronic tablet.

SALTFLEETBY showing the station buildings, signal box and running-in board in early **British Railways** days. *Douglas Thompson.*

SALTFLEETBY as it was except for the addition of the single-storey building to the left of the main house.

Immingham based class B1 4-6-0 No 61098 arrives at Grimoldby station in the late 1950s. Built in November 1946 No 61098 was withdrawn in July 1965. The station is in good order and a siding can be seen behind the platform. *Douglas Thompson.*

This is Grimoldby today. It was the first station out of Louth on the Louth to Mablethorpe line. It was once the home of the actor Donald Pleasence, whose father was stationmaster here between 1929 and 1933.

Boston based class J2 0-6-0 No 65017 leaving Mumby Road with a Mablethorpe-Nottingham Victoria holiday express on 30th August 1951. The train is using the "summer only" passing loop at Mumby Road, normally all services used the platform line. *J. Cupit.*

MUMBY ROAD station site today seen here from the B1149 overbridge with the splendid stationmaster's house on the left. A similar building still exists at Sutton on Sea.

Mumby Road station is mentioned in the well-known song by Flanders and Swann, "Slow Train" - a lament for the loss of many loved stations and lines in the 1960s. 'Dogdyke' and Tumby Woodside' are also mentioned.

Miller's Dale for Tideswell ...
Kirby Muxloe ...
Mow Cop and Scholar Green ...

No more will I go to Blandford Forum and Mortehoe
On the slow train from Midsomer Norton and Mumby Road.
No churns, no porter, no cat on a seat
At Chorlton-cum-Hardy or Chester-le-Street.
We won't be meeting again
On the Slow Train.

I'll travel no more from Littleton Badsey to Openshaw.
At Long Stanton I'll stand well clear of the doors no more.
No whitewashed pebbles, no Up and no Down
From Formby Four Crosses to Dunstable Town.
I won't be going again
On the Slow Train.

On the Main Line and the Goods Siding
The grass grows high
At Dog Dyke, Tumby Woodside
And Trouble House Halt.

The Sleepers sleep at Audlem and Ambergate.
No passenger waits on Chittening platform or Cheslyn Hay.
No one departs, no one arrives
From Selby to Goole, from St Erth to St Ives.
They've all passed out of our lives
On the Slow Train, on the Slow Train.

Cockermouth for Buttermere ... on the Slow Train,
Armley Moor Arram ...
Pye Hill and Somercotes ... on the Slow Train,
Windmill End.

Courtesy of the Michael Flanders Estate.

The New Line

THE KIRKSTEAD AND LITTLE STEEPING RAILWAY was better known as the New Line. It was a latecomer, being built by a Light Railway Order and opened on 1st July 1913. It provided a more direct route between Lincoln and Skegness than that via Boston. The line closed on Saturday 3rd October 1970.

NEW BOLINGBROKE village was founded by John Parkinson, steward of Sir Joseph Banks. The new settlement was 7 miles south south west of Old Bolingbroke and was sited so that it could have water communication with Boston and the surrounding fen by means of navigable drains.

Harold Squires recalled the large number of excursion trains, "which used to thunder through the station at weekends on their way to Skegness from the Midlands. There were also cheap excursions from the villages at weekends costing one shilling return to Skegness.

In July scores of horses would arrive at the station from where they would be walked to Revesby Park, ready for the Revesby Show. The arrival of the horses was a great occasion for us children, we sat on the grass and watched the proceedings.

My father used to send his Rhode Island Red poultry to various shows throughout the country, via the station. When they returned we used to search the hampers to see if they contained any prize cards. They were sometimes half-eaten by the prize winner!"

A pick-up goods train at New Bolingbroke circa 1914. The waiting shelters have their wooden canopies in place, in later years they were removed. *Harness Rundle.*

Porter Frank Redman in his uniform and with a very substantial trolley, with the level crossing and New Bolingbroke signal box behind him in GNR days. The flat nature of the surrounding countryside is well shown.

NEW BOLINGBROKE Booking Office is similar to others along the New Line. It is now functioning as an antiques shop with the appropriate name 'Junktion'.

MIDVILLE village is situated in the centre of East Fen, the station was north of the village, alongside a minor road which follows the course of Hobhole Drain. The red brick station buildings here were identical to others along the line, however the platforms were of wooden construction, the same as those at Coningsby.

To the west of the station, beyond the level crossing and the drain, a 369 yard long refuge siding was provided. During World War 2 GNR Pullman carriages were stored in the siding to get them away from Hornsey carriage sidings in London. This was a busy station dealing with the usual farm produce, particularly potatoes and sugar beet. It was also popular with anglers from the Sheffield area who came by train at weekends to fish Hobhole Drain.

MIDVILLE station in 1970, Hobhole Drain is in the foreground, the level crossing, the ubiquitous booking office, signal box and waiting room beyond. *Peter Grey.*

A GNR oil lamp at Midville station in 1970. *P. Anderson.*

MIDVILLE Booking Office is little changed from the original photo, the sign above the door announcing 'Old Station Building'. It stands across the road from Hobhole Drain, the abutments of the bridge which carried the railway over the drain are seen in the picture below.

TUMBY WOODSIDE STATION station served a few houses scattered along an unclassified road. The signal box, similar to others on the line, was built with a shallow pitched roof and tall operating floor windows typical of the late GNR style. Signalmen included Jess Carrot, Bill Burrows and later, Archie Blagg, who came to Tumby Woodside after being a telegraph lad at Spring Lane, and remained until the end.

The station did considerable business in cattle, potatoes and sugar beet, local users included Messrs Sinclair & Co of Mareham-le-Fen, millers and general farm merchants who received all their offals and cake by rail from Grimsby and Hull.

Leaking steam, class J11/3 0-6-0 No 64346 works through Tumby Woodside with a Lincoln, Holmes Yard, to Firsby Pick-up goods train on 19th June 1961. Beyond the superb lattice GNR somersault signal is the generously proportioned stationmaster's house. *D. B. Swale.*

The station booking office at Tumby Woodside, on 13th August 1970, was typical of those along the line. *G. Goslin.*

TUMBY WOODSIDE Booking Office is the same style as those at Midville and New Bolingbroke, now a private residence.

Some of the station buildings still survive at Tumby Woodside. The platforms cannot be seen, but they are there, hidden in the undergrowth.